A LION CALLED CHRISTIAN

Anthony Bourke & John Rendall

LEVEL 4

Adapted by: Jane Revell

Publisher: Jacquie Bloese

Editor: Cheryl Pelteret

Cover layout: Eddie Rego

Designer: Sylvia Tate

Picture research: Pupak Navabpour

Photo credits:

Cover: © Derek Cattani

Pages 4–76: © Derek Cattani for the Born Free Foundation and the George Adamson Wildlife Preservation Trust.

Pages 9, 11 & 26: M Hibberd/Getty Images; A Messer/Rex Features, UK21/Alamy.

Page 77: K McKay/Rex Features.

Pages 78 & 79: D Kitwood, R Elliot/AFP/Getty Images; S Cardinale/Corbis; C Radburn/PA Photos.

Pages 80 & 81: R Harding, T Walker, AFP/Getty Images; R Jones/Rex Features.

Pages 82 & 83: Hulton Archive/Getty Images; B Moody/Rex Features.

Printed in Singapore

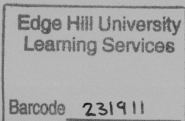

CONTENTS

PAGE

PEOPLE

ANTHONY 'ACE' BOURKE AND JOHN RENDALL were young Australian friends in their twenties. They left Australia to travel around Europe. In London, in 1969, they bought a lion cub called Christian.

GEORGE ADAMSON lived in Kenya for most of his life. He and his wife, Joy, rescued many lions and returned them to the wild.

BILL TRAVERS AND VIRGINIA MCKENNA played the parts of George and Joy Adamson in the film *Born Free*. After the film, both worked hard to protect animals in the wild.

LIONS

CHRISTIAN

Christian and his three sisters were born in a zoo in England in August, 1969. Two of his sisters were sent to a circus, but Christian and another sister were bought by Harrods.

PLACES

LONDON

'Sophistocat' was a furniture shop in the King's Road, Chelsea, in the 1960s. Ace and John had a flat above the shop and it was Christian's first 'home'.

Harrods is the most famous department store in London. It also used to have a zoo with wild animals for sale.

LEITH HILL is about 50 km from London. Bill Travers and Virginia McKenna had a house here. Christian spent about three months here before he went to Africa.

KAMPI YA SIMBA, KORA, KENYA is where Christian was returned to the wild. Kora is a dry, empty part of Kenya, 450 kilometres north-east of Nairobi. Kampi ya Simba means 'the camp of the lions'.

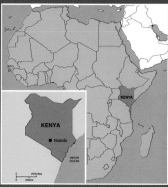

BOY AND KATANIA

Boy was an angry seven-year-old male lion. Katania was a sweet four-month-old lioness. Both lions had been rescued by George and he hoped to return them to the wild with Christian.

PROLOGUE

In 2006, a Californian student posted a video on *YouTube*, the popular video-sharing website. The video was taken from a very old film from 1971, and everyone who saw it on *YouTube* loved it. It touched people in different ways. Many of them sent it to their friends. Over the months, the video was watched and enjoyed by millions and millions of people all over the world. So why was this three-minute video so extraordinary?

In the video, we see two young men standing on a rock somewhere in the wild African countryside. The men have long hair and are in their twenties. They are waiting for someone or something. Then suddenly a large male lion appears from behind a rock. The lion looks at them. It starts to run towards them – and then the most amazing thing happens. The lion jumps up on the two young men,

Christian's reunion with Ace and John, 1971

and hugs them, licking their faces. The men put their arms around the lion and hug it back, laughing. They are obviously very pleased to see the lion, and the lion is very pleased to see them.

The lion was called Christian. The two young men were Australians, Anthony ('Ace') Bourke and John Rendall. It may seem unbelievable, but the lion knew the two men very well. Although Christian hadn't seen John and Ace for a year, he still remembered who they were. He knew that they were his old friends.

This is the story of that lion, and how Ace and John came to own him. It's the story of how Christian lived with Ace and John in their small flat in London and of how they became friends and grew to love and trust one another. It's the story of how, when Christian got too big to look after, Ace and John had to find a new home for him. They didn't want to put him in a zoo or a circus – that would be like a prison for Christian. They wanted a home for him where he could be happy and free. So the story tells us how Christian was finally able to return to Kenya and live with other lions in the wild.

Ace and John first wrote *A Lion Called Christian* in 1971, the year of their reunion with him in Africa. In 2009, they rewrote the book, after the *YouTube* video had brought the story to the attention of a much wider audience.

In the Introduction to the 2009 book, the writers ask themselves why the *YouTube* video is so popular. Is it just because people are able to see an unusual reunion and share a very special experience? Or is there more to it than that? Is it because a wild animal seems to be showing its feelings? Is it about growing up and leaving home? Is it about losing someone and finding them again? Is it about the relationship we have with our own pets? Or perhaps it's because we miss being part of the natural world, now that technology and computer games have taken us further away from it?

Whatever the reason, one thing is true: the Internet has completely changed how we communicate with each other. We can give and receive information, meet other people, download music and films, buy and sell things, play games … we can do almost anything. The Internet has also made it possible for us to work for the things we believe in. We can join others who are fighting against climate change or helping to save animals in danger, for example. We can work together to face some of the big problems in the world that affect us all.

CHAPTER 1
A LION FOR SALE

Harrods, London

In August, 1969, four lion cubs were born in a small zoo in the south-west of England. There were three females and a male. Their father, Butch, came from Rotterdam Zoo in the Netherlands and their mother, Mary, from a zoo in Jerusalem, Israel. In October, when the summer was over and the tourists had gone, the cubs were sold. Two of the females were bought by a circus. The other female and the male were bought by Harrods, a very famous department store in London.

Three months earlier, in May, 1969, two young Australian men, Anthony ('Ace') Bourke and John Rendall, had left Australia for the first time. They had finished university and had done a number of jobs. After travelling on their own around Europe in search of adventure, Ace and John met up again in London. They visited the usual tourist attractions like the Tower of London, and then, one day, they went to Harrods.

Harrods was a very special department store. The owners of Harrods used to proudly say that the store offered 'all things, for all people, everywhere'. At that time, there was even a zoo in the shop. Ace and John wanted to see if they really could buy 'anything' in Harrods. They went to the zoo on the second floor to see the animals for sale. And there, in a small cage between the cats and the dogs, they saw the two lion cubs.

The female cub seemed bad-tempered and showed her teeth to shoppers who stopped to look at her. Her brother seemed quite easy-going. He didn't pay attention to anybody. Ace and John immediately fell in love with him. They sat down beside the cage and stayed there for hours.

'I've already named him Christian,' said Ace.

Ace and John both laughed. It would be amusing to call a lion Christian. It reminded them of Roman history, when Christians were thrown to the lions.

'Why don't we buy him?' asked John.

They asked if the cub was still for sale. Yes, he was, they were told, at a price of £275. At that time, this was a lot of money but the price didn't stop Ace and John. They really wanted to buy the lion cub.

But first the manager of the Harrods zoo department wanted to interview them. He wanted to make sure they would be good lion owners. So the next day, Ace and

John got out their smart jackets. Luckily, their parents had made them take the jackets with them to Europe! Up to now, they had never been worn. Then they carefully combed their hair and went back to Harrods. Luckily, the interview went well and the zoo manager liked them. But their problems were only just beginning.

Ace and John shared a small flat above a furniture shop called 'Sophistocat' in the King's Road, in Chelsea. This part of Chelsea was called World's End. The name came from the seventeenth century, in the days of King Charles II, when this area was right at the end of the city. Now, the area at the end of the King's Road was becoming very fashionable.

King's Road, Chelsea, 1970

Ace and John had to wait three weeks before they could take Christian home, so they only had a short time to find a larger flat. What they really needed was a big basement flat with a garden. They didn't want to tell flat owners that they had a lion so they said they were looking for a flat for themselves and their 'dog'! In the end, when they couldn't find a suitable flat, they put an advertisement in *The Times* newspaper.

LION CUB, 2 young men, need suitable garden/roof, flat/house, London.

However, the only calls they received were from newspapers who were interested in taking photos of the lion cub. Nobody called to offer them a flat to live in.

In the end, the owners of 'Sophistocat' agreed to let Christian live in the large basement under the shop. The basement had several rooms, so there was plenty of space for Christian to move around. Ace and John thought 'Sophisto*cat*' was a very suitable address for a lion – the biggest cat of all! But they still had to find a garden for Christian to exercise in. Finally they were told that they could use a large church garden, close to their flat.

Now they were ready to receive Christian. But they still had one problem. Neither of them knew anything about lions! They had no idea how to look after a lion. Would they be able to do it?

They went to Harrods as often as they could to play with the cubs for an hour after closing time. They wanted to get to know Christian and to let him get to know them. The cubs had extremely sharp teeth and claws. Ace and John hoped that Christian would play more quietly when he was away from his sister.

They also went to visit some people who had bought a puma from Harrods the year before. The puma, called Margot, seemed quite relaxed and Ace and John felt a bit more confident about looking after Christian.

They knew, however, that Christian would only be able to live with them for about six months. After that, he would be too big for their basement. They had to think about possibilities for him when he was fully grown. They certainly didn't want to send him back to a zoo. They knew of a place in the south of England called Longleat Safari Park. Longleat was the first safari park to open outside Africa. Animals were not kept in cages: instead, they were allowed to move around the large park. The lions at Longleat seemed to have a large amount of freedom. Ace and John went to visit Longleat and talked to the director.

'Don't worry,' said the director. 'We'll take Christian when he gets too big for you to keep.'

So everything was arranged, even Christian's future. But Ace and John still had doubts. Christian was a powerful wild animal. He could be very dangerous. Their parents were worried and told them to think about it very carefully. They said that Ace and John could become attached to Christian and they might find it difficult to give him up. A lot of people told them they were stupid, or crazy. In the end, all these different opinions only made Ace and John's decision easier. They were young and they were looking for fun and adventure. It was the end of the 1960s and the beginning of the 1970s: a time of optimism and change. They would buy a lion and live with him in London.

On 15th December, 1969, there was a phone call from Harrods. The cubs had escaped during the night. They had done some damage in the store. Harrods wanted to get rid of Christian and his sister … as soon as possible!

'Right. We'll be there tomorrow,' Ace and John said.

CHAPTER 2
'A LION IN CHELSEA? IMPOSSIBLE!'

When Ace and John arrived to collect Christian from
Harrods, everything went smoothly at first. Sitting in
the back seat of their car, the young lion looked calm
and thoughtful. But as the car began to move, he became
nervous. After spending all his life in a cage, he must have
found being in a car very confusing. He jumped around
from seat to seat. Ace and John couldn't make him sit
quietly. They stopped the car often and gave him a big
soft toy to play with – a 'welcome home' present – but he
wasn't interested.

Eventually they got home and carried Christian into
the shop below their flat where their friends were waiting.
Ace and John stayed up most of the night and played with
him. Christian was theirs at last.

A lion in the King's Road in Chelsea was not too
surprising in those days. In the 1960s and early 70s, there
was always something extraordinary to see in this part of
London. It was where many famous designers, musicians,
artists, photographers, writers and singers lived. People
like the Beatles and the Rolling Stones were often seen
there in the fashionable clothes shops, restaurants, clubs
and markets. Wild animals as pets were part of this
unusual crowd – a couple of other people owned big, wild
cats.

Christian quickly got used to his new home. He enjoyed
being with Ace and John. He loved to be carried and
hugged, and he liked to put his paws around them and
lick their faces. He was very playful, and within two days
he had torn his new soft toy into pieces.

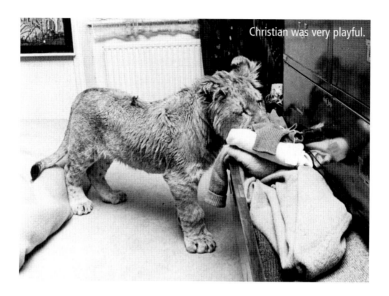
Christian was very playful.

His day began at 8 am when Ace or John came downstairs. Christian was very sleepy, and sometimes they even had to wake him up. He was always pleased to see them. The first thing he did was use his toilet box in the corner of the room. After a few 'mistakes' at the beginning, he had learned to use it very easily.

Then it was time for breakfast: a mixture of baby foods and milk. He ate the same food for his dinner, too. For his other two meals, late in the morning and in the early evening, he had uncooked meat and an egg. Ace and John knew a French cook who sometimes brought Christian delicious steaks. With four meals a day and such good food, Christian quickly grew bigger and bigger. Every week he needed more meat and became more expensive to feed.

'It's a pity he isn't a vegetarian!' joked Ace and John.

When he wasn't eating, Christian loved to play. He played with lots of different toys: bones and rubber balls and soft toys … none of the toys lasted more than two minutes before they were torn apart. Christian's favourite toys were bins. He used to wear one on his head, over his eyes so that he couldn't see anything. Then he used to take it off and tear it into pieces. He loved attention. If Ace or John were reading or talking on the phone, he used to climb onto them. Christian liked to play in the shop too. He liked to follow Ace and John secretly and hide behind

Christian and his favourite toy

things, as though he was hunting.

Ace and John were very careful not to allow Christian to jump on them. They didn't want him to realize that he was much stronger than them. If he played too roughly with them, they always stopped the game. They didn't want him to know that he could harm them by accident.

Most of the shop's customers were surprised, but very happy, to see Christian in the shop. They often came back on Saturdays with their husbands and children or their friends. It sometimes meant that there were too many people in the shop at one time, and Christian had to spend the day in the basement.

Every afternoon, Ace and John took Christian to the church garden for an hour. It wasn't far away, and at first they tried to lead him along the pavement like a dog, but it was too difficult. Sometimes he ran and pulled them along behind them. Sometimes he sat down and refused to move. He was frightened of all the cars and people. When he was very young, they could carry him in their arms, but as he grew, he got too heavy, so they had to drive him to the garden in the car.

The garden was perfect. There were no other people or animals there, and all around it was a high stone wall. There was a large area of grass for Christian to play on, and trees and bushes to hide behind. In the beginning, Christian was scared to go out into the centre of the garden. He needed the protection of the bushes. Ace and John thought it would be a bad idea to let him get used to chasing them. So they kicked footballs for him to chase instead. Christian loved the game and he was very fast. He ran after the ball, jumped on it and turned over and over with it on the grass. There were a few days of snow that winter. Christian loved that too and didn't mind the cold.

Football in the church garden

Christian liked to sit on top of furniture in the shop and watch everything from a great height. He used to sit in the shop window, like a lion king! People who walked past in the street stopped to stare at him. Motorists stopped too, which sometimes led to accidents with other cars! Christian was such an attraction that the police asked Ace and John not to let him sit in the window on days when there was a football match at the nearby Chelsea football ground*. 'There might be problems amongst the football crowd, ' the police said.

Someone once heard a young child on a passing bus say to his mother: 'Mummy, there was a lion in that shop window!'

'A lion in Chelsea? Impossible!' said the child's mother. 'Stop telling lies.'

Looking at the customers in 'Sophistocat'

* Chelsea is a popular London football team.

CHAPTER 3
LIVING WITH A LION

Ace and John were lucky. Harrods had sold them a wonderful lion. He was healthy and he had a fantastic personality. He wasn't frightened easily and he didn't get angry. He seemed to trust them and feel safe with them. Surprisingly, he was much easier to live with than they had expected. They were able to establish a very good relationship with him: one built on love and respect.

In some ways, he was very 'human'. He liked to have fun. If he fell over something – which he often did with his big paws – he seemed to be embarrassed. Then, like humans often do, he quickly pretended that nothing had happened.

Christian always looked forward to seeing the cleaner who came to clean the shop every day. She soon got used to having to do the housework with a lion running after her, trying to take her cleaning materials away or ride on the machine as she was hoovering.

Christian was a very good judge of people. He could tell if a person was uncomfortable with him or afraid of him. If they were nervous, he liked to frighten them a little bit, by hiding away and then making a noise, just for fun. His favourite place to sit was on the stairs leading from the shop to the upstairs flat. He hated being ignored. If customers didn't notice him, he used to knock their hat or glasses off with his paw.

Christian found children interesting. He seemed to know that they were different from adults. Perhaps it was because he was about the same height as a small child! Once, he accidentally knocked a child over as he was

Christian's favourite place

trying to say hello. Luckily, the child wasn't hurt, and although the mother was cross at first, she came back to 'Sophistocat' the next day, bringing lots of children with her to meet Christian!

He was a very handsome lion, with a soft, golden coat. But the most beautiful thing about him were his eyes. They were big, warm and brown, and he used them to communicate many different things. He was also a very intelligent animal, with a good memory. He very quickly learned how to open the door of the basement, or to find his food on top of a high cupboard and knock it down to the floor so that he could eat it.

For lions, family is very important. Ace and John were Christian's family. They gave him a lot of affection and he showed them lots of affection in return. Lions greet each other by touching heads so Ace and John always got down on their knees to let Christian do this to them. He sometimes greeted them by standing up on his back legs and hugging them. That was always a big surprise. No one had ever seen a lion do that before!

Christian's behaviour with food was also unusual for a lion. Lions are generally very 'jealous' about their food. They will attack anyone who tries to take it away. Christian loved his food and often knocked it out of his owners' hands before they had time to put it on the floor for him. But he didn't mind if they tried to take it away. He was so gentle, they could even take it out of his mouth.

A lion uses his mouth to communicate as well as to eat. When Christian licked them to show affection, Ace and John could feel his rough tongue. They sometimes felt his teeth too, which were very sharp. He quickly learned not to bite them, but unfortunately his mouth was often open … at knee height! As a result, Ace and John had several pairs of trousers, torn at the knee.

Christian also had sharp claws and – like any cat – he needed to exercise them. The table and chair legs in the shop were perfect for this. He damaged a few very expensive pieces of furniture in the first few weeks, until he learned to exercise his claws on the stairs instead.

After the claw-exercising problems of the first few weeks, he only damaged a piece of furniture if he fell off it by accident. One day, there was a very expensive table in the middle of the shop. On it were plates, knives, forks and glasses, all beautifully placed. Christian was lying on top of the table too, and when he moved his weight to one side, the table and everything on it fell to the floor. Christian pushed his claws into the table top and held on. There were claw marks all over the table. As the table had already been sold, Ace and John had to phone the lady who had bought it. They wanted to apologise.

'Don't worry,' she said. 'I only came into the shop to see your beautiful lion, and then I saw that beautiful table! The damage will remind me of Christian.'

Christian's best friend was a young woman called Unity. When Unity heard there was a lion at 'Sophistocat', she came to the shop immediately to meet him. Unity loved lions. She had owned a lion called Lola when she lived in Italy. She and Lola had had to move house twenty times in search of a suitable place to live, so Unity understood what it was like to live with a lion. Unity was very small and very slim but she wasn't afraid of Christian. She came to visit him every day and they used to play for hours in the basement.

When Christian heard her footsteps at the door, he always stopped playing with his ball or toy to listen and try to work out who was there. When he heard Unity say, 'Hello, Christian! I've come to play!' he used to run to the basement door to wait for her. When she opened the door, he pulled her by her coat and led her into the basement to play.

In all the months Christian lived at 'Sophistocat', there was only one time when Ace and John were frightened of him. Christian had found a belt made of animal skin in the shop and had run down into the basement with it. When Ace and John tried to take the belt away from him, Christian suddenly became angry. He made his ears flat against his head, and pulled back his lips to show his teeth. Ace and John knew that he might attack them if they tried to take the belt away again. They moved away, making sure he didn't know they were afraid of him. They didn't want him to realise how powerful he was. He was a lion, after all, and could be dangerous. They certainly didn't want to try to train him like a circus animal, or stop him from following his natural instincts. But the occasion was a warning to them that one day, the time would come when they might not be able to manage Christian any more.

CHAPTER 4
'ARE LIONS ALLOWED?'

It's hard to keep it a secret when you have a lion as a pet, and Christian soon became famous. It wasn't long before he was invited to be 'interviewed' on BBC Radio.

When Ace and John arrived at the BBC, the guard stopped them and said: 'Sorry. There's a rule here – no dogs are allowed.'

'What about lions?' they asked. 'Are lions allowed?' To this, the guard had no reply, and he had to let them in.

The interview

The interviewer was hoping that Christian would roar on the radio. Unfortunately for the listeners, Christian was shy of the microphone and remained completely silent for the whole interview!

Christian was also invited to appear on a children's

TV programme. This time he was confused by the bright lights and frightened of the cameras. Ace or John spent a lot of time on the floor with Christian, trying to stop him from running away. Luckily, people watching the programme afterwards thought they were watching a man and a lion playing together!

After the TV programme there was a lot of interest in Christian. Magazines and newspapers wanted to take photos of him. But they wanted him to look wild and frightening. They took photos of him in the middle of a yawn, when his mouth was wide open and his teeth were showing. They wanted their readers to think he was a dangerous lion. Ace and John decided they needed to be more careful about the photographs that appeared in the newspapers. They met a photographer called Derek Cattani who understood Christian. They asked Derek to take photos of him. After that, if the newspapers wanted photos, they had to buy them from Derek.

Ace and John agreed to let Christian appear in some advertisements, as long as he enjoyed them. He was getting very expensive to feed, and Ace and John needed the extra money from the advertising. In one photo, Christian is seen sitting with six tiny new-born chickens. Nobody could believe how gentle he was with them! In another advertisement, for top fashion magazine *Vanity Fair*, Christian had to lie on

Christian and the chickens

25

a bed with a beautiful actress. The actress had lovely long hair. Christian always enjoyed chewing hair. However, the actress did *not* enjoy it, and Christian had to stop. He was cross about this – so he bit a hole in the bed cover instead and destroyed the expensive pillows!

Sometimes on Sundays, when the shop was closed, Ace and John took Christian out. Unfortunately there aren't many places in London that you can take a lion. Once they

The lions at Trafalgar Square

drove him to Trafalgar Square to see the four lions at the bottom of Nelson's Column. He enjoyed that very much.

Another time they took him to a park called Kensington Gardens but he was frightened by the big open space. Lots of people came up and stared at him too and he didn't like that at all.

One day Ace and John took him to a children's home. They thought it would be a nice surprise for the children to see a lion. The director kept Christian in one room, while the children had afternoon tea with Ace and John in another room. But one of the children opened the door to Christian's room and he ran to find Ace and John. The children screamed and jumped onto chairs and tables. Christian had never seen people behave like that before. He went home, very quiet and confused – while the children probably had nightmares for a long time afterwards.

Sometimes Ace and John took Christian with them when they were invited to their friends' houses. On one visit Christian pushed open a bathroom door. There was a loud scream. It was difficult to know who was more frightened – the girl sitting in the bath, or Christian himself!

Ace and John often went to visit their friends who owned the puma, Margot. They hoped that Margot and Christian would become friends. But Margot was a different kind of big cat; she was also older than Christian, and very jealous of him. Margot didn't like Christian at all. The only time he went near her, she hit him on the nose with her paw. He didn't go near her again.

As Christian became more and more famous, and articles about him appeared in newspapers all over the world, Ace and John received lots of phone calls and letters about him. But only one letter attacked them for owning a lion. In April, 1970, a woman in the USA wrote to them. Her letter ended:

> That lion must be quite big now. You have made him live an unnatural life – he must be bored and unhappy. You have probably pulled out his claws and his teeth. A zoo won't want him without claws and teeth. So what are you going to do with him when you get bored? Have you thought about his future?

The woman was wrong about Christian's life. Ace and John had not pulled out his claws or teeth, and Christian wasn't unhappy. But she had been right to question their plans for his future. Ace and John had been worried about it for some time now. What *were* they going to do with him?

CHAPTER 5
DINNER WITH A FILM DIRECTOR

Christian was getting bored. By April, 1970, he was eight months old and weighed about sixty kilograms. He was too big to sit on the stairs anymore. It was too easy for him to climb over the furniture in the shop. When he sat in the shop window, he frightened people away, so he had to spend most of his time in the basement.

Ace and John were worried. They watched as the paw prints Christian left on the windows and doors grew higher and higher. They couldn't give him the freedom he needed. But they knew that if he was bored, he could become dangerous.

They went back to Longleat, the Safari Park they had visited once before. But this time they knew more about lions and they saw everything differently. They discovered that the animals at Longleat were often hired by film and television companies or lent to a circus. They decided that Longleat was not the right place for Christian after all. They didn't want to send him to a zoo either. What other choices were there?

One afternoon, the actor, Bill Travers and his wife, actress Virginia McKenna, came into the shop. They had been the stars of the famous 1966 film *Born Free*, which told the true story of a lioness cub. The cub, whose parents had been killed, had been rescued in Kenya by a couple called Joy and George Adamson, and they had returned her to the wild.

Bill and Virginia had learned a lot about lions from their acting experience in *Born Free*. Since the 1966 film, they had worked hard to protect wild animals and they had

Virginia McKenna and Bill Travers meet Christian.

made a lot of TV and radio programmes on the subject.
They were against the buying and selling of wild animals.
But they were glad that Ace and John had rescued
Christian from a life in a cage. They were amazed to see a
lion that showed such affection.

Ace and John told them their worries about Christian's
future. A few days later Bill came back to 'Sophistocat'
with the director of *Born Free,* James Hill. Ace and John
wondered why James was asking them so many questions
about Christian. They were surprised and excited when
Bill invited them to dinner at his house in the country.

Dinner with famous film stars! The people at World's
End watched in amazement as Ace and John were
collected by James – in a smart Rolls-Royce*. They were

* A Rolls-Royce is a very expensive British car.

driven to Bill and Virginia's country house. After dinner they watched a film Bill had made called *The Lions Are Free*. It was about three lions who had been returned to the wild after the filming of *Born Free*. Bill's film showed what had happened when he visited those lions several years later. The lions hadn't seen Bill for three years but they remembered him! And they ran up and greeted him with great affection.

The film ended with Virginia visiting a zoo to see another lioness from the film *Born Free*. When Virginia called the lioness's name, it ran up to her. But with a fence separating them, they couldn't touch heads to say hello like they used to. It was very sad to watch. Ace and John thought about Christian. Would this happen to him too?

Bill knew what they were thinking. He turned to them and said. 'I think we can help you with the problem of Christian's future. We would like to fly Christian out to Africa so that George Adamson can try to return him to the wild.'

Bill explained that after their meeting in 'Sophistocat', he had contacted George in Kenya and told him about Christian. George was very interested in the idea of bringing a lion from England and returning it to the wild in Africa. He was confident it would be successful. But it would be expensive, so Bill and James wanted to make a film about Christian called *A Lion at World's End*. This would help to pay for the project.

Ace and John thought it was a brilliant idea. On the way back to London they spoke excitedly about Christian's future. How lucky they had been to meet Bill and Virginia! They knew there would be lots of dangers for Christian in the African countryside. It was possible that his life as a city lion would make it difficult for him to

John (left) and Ace with Christian

become wild again. They also knew that lions can live for eighteen or twenty years in zoos, but they don't normally survive more than ten to twelve years in the wild. On the other hand, Christian would escape a long, safe but boring life in a cage. He would be given the chance to live where he belonged – in Africa.

That night, as if to celebrate his luck, Christian made his first attempt at a real roar. It seemed the right way to start a new adventure.

CHAPTER 6
'THE LION AT WORLD'S END'

A few days later, Bill Travers flew to Kenya for discussions with the Kenyan government about making the TV programme. He was optimistic that the government would say yes to the suggestion. The programme would be a good advertisement for Kenya and help attract more tourists. He also knew that African governments at the time wanted to show the world that they thought the protection of animals was important.

On the other hand, lions have always been a natural enemy for Africans, and one of George Adamson's lions had recently hurt a child. Some people in the Kenyan government were against returning lions to the wild. They believed that lions which were used to being with humans were a problem. They might easily go up to people in game parks and the results could be very dangerous.

After a lot of discussion, the Kenyan government finally agreed: Christian could come to Kenya if a suitable place could be found. The area had to have water and enough wild animals so that the lions could hunt for food. It also had to be somewhere where there were no tourists or farmers and their animals. George began to search for an area which fitted the government's description. Bill returned to England and made plans to begin filming the following week.

James Hill would direct the film, called *The Lion at World's End.* It would start with Bill and Virginia's first meeting with Christian and then record the story exactly as it happened. The idea was to bring people's attention to the protection of wild animals. James told Ace and John to wear their most fashionable clothes and not to cut their long, seventies-style hair. Ace and John said that they felt embarrassed about their appearance in the years that followed!

As the shop was going to be closed for two days for filming, it would lose money. So Ace and John decided to do something generous for the owners. On Sunday, the day before filming began, they repainted the shop walls white. It took them all day. They were just finishing, when Christian knocked the paint tin over. Christian was so surprised that he jumped back and fell over. Then he ran to the other end of the shop. There were white paw marks all over the black floor. Christian himself was covered in white paint – and he was going to be in a film the next day!

Ace and John spent a long time that night washing the paint off Christian – who thought it was a great new game – and repainting the floor.

The next day 'Sophistocat' was filled with lots of people and equipment and bright lights. Christian was confused by it all, but this made him quieter and he co-operated well. Bill was very pleased with Christian's acting ability. Ace and John's voices, however, had to be re-recorded by Australian actors, because Bill thought Ace and John sounded 'too English'!

The second day's filming didn't go quite so well. They were filming in the church garden. This was Christian's special garden and he didn't want to share it with all those people. He normally loved chasing footballs, but that day he refused to co-operate. He didn't like the noise of the slow-motion camera either. He stopped moving as soon as he heard it. In the end, Ace and John broke their rule about letting Christian chase them. It was the only way to get him to run. They ran, and he chased after them. This was the game that he had always wanted to play – he couldn't believe his luck! Ace and John went home, their clothes destroyed, but at least Bill had a good piece of film.

Several days later, they all watched the film taken on those first two days. Christian looked wonderful and the slow-motion parts were amazing. None of them had ever seen a lion in slow-motion before. For the first time they were really able to see how strong and powerful he was, and how perfectly he moved.

But that was the last time Christian was able to exercise in the church garden during the day. Other people were starting to use the garden, too, and Christian was getting too big and scary. The time Christian refused to climb

Christian leaves London.

down from the roof of a car didn't help things … . Ace and John were told that they could take Christian to the garden only very early in the morning, at 6.30 am. This meant Christian had no afternoon trip to look forward to. He had to spend the rest of the day in the basement.

Then Bill and Virginia made a suggestion. They would build a compound for Christian in their large garden at their house in the country. Ace and John could live there with Christian until it was time to go to Kenya.

When the compound was ready, Christian left the King's Road and London forever. Many of his World's End friends came to say goodbye and to watch him leave. It was a sad moment. Ace and John knew that the five happy months they had spent with Christian in London were finally over.

CHAPTER 7
COUNTRY LIFE

Bill and Virginia's house at Leith Hill was only fifty kilometres from London, but it was in the middle of the countryside. And it had a perfect English garden, green and full of flowers – not the natural home for an African lion, but Christian ran around, exploring happily.

Christian's caravan, Leith Hill

He seemed to like his compound too. It measured twenty-five metres by fifteen metres and had a tall tree and several bushes in it. It also had a colourful caravan.

Christian was so excited that the first thing he did was climb the tree. But he had never climbed a tree before, so he didn't know how to get down. He just sat there, waiting for Ace and John to help him.

That night Ace and John were asked to sell Christian. For the price of £500, he now belonged to the film company that had made *A Lion at World's End*. Ace and John felt guilty about selling Christian, but they preferred to think of him as belonging to Kenya, rather than to a film company.

Bill thought that Christian would enjoy sleeping outside that night, but Ace and John were sure Christian would prefer the caravan. They were right, of course. Ace and John slept in another caravan beside the compound. The next morning Christian greeted them very happily; he must have worried that they might have returned to London during the night and left him alone.

Ace and John expected to stay at Leith Hill for only a few weeks but there were delays. George had suggested two possible areas to the Kenyan government but they had not been accepted. Luckily the summer weather was pleasant and Ace and John could spend the days reading, sunbathing and playing with Christian in his compound. Christian was very happy, too. His life was less complicated than in London and he had more freedom. He began to live more like a lion in the wild, sleeping during the day while it was hot, and becoming more active in the cooler evening time.

Bill and Virginia had three young children and several dogs. Christian liked to watch the children from his

John playing with Christian at Leith Hill

compound. He wanted to play with them, but he couldn't get out. Unless Ace and John were with him, he walked up and down his compound again and again. He wasn't very interested in the dogs, but if one of them came too close to the compound, he always got down and lay with his ears flat … ready to jump on them. He thought no one could see him, but he forgot about his tail. It always moved quickly from side to side in excitement. Ace and John were pleased to see this natural lion behaviour. It would make it easier for Christian to return to the wild.

Christian was a big lion but he needed to be as strong as possible for his new life. Ace and John hung a large 'attack' bag from the tree in Christian's compound. Christian loved to attack it. He often hung on to it with all four legs off the ground. This was good practice for Kenya. It helped to make him stronger and his claws sharper. He had a different diet, too – sometimes he ate the whole head or stomach of a sheep or other animal Ace and John had bought from the meat market.

'What on earth are you feeding – a crocodile?' joked the man at the market.

Christian had never been to the beach, so one day Bill decided it would be a great idea to take him there and do some filming. Ace and John didn't agree. It meant leaving at 3 am and it was a hundred kilometres there and back. When they got to the beach, it was grey and empty, but the dawn was beautiful. Christian was too scared to go in the sea, but the film showed him running with Bill, Ace and John along the beach. As they drove home, they wondered what people on the beach would think later when they saw a lion's paw prints on the sand!

Days became weeks, and weeks became months. James Hill, the film director, came down to continue filming several times. Ace and John spent most of the time trying to stop Christian from jumping on James. He said he only wanted to protect 'his new trousers' from Christian's sharp claws, but he seemed to wear 'new trousers' every day … Unity came down from London two or three days a week. She loved spending the day with Christian and discovering new games to play with him. With Unity and with everyone else, Christian always played very gently, except on rainy days, when the weather affected him. He always became quite wild when it rained. On those days Ace and John stayed outside the compound.

Christian tried a new trick: if he jumped up and held

Christian at Leith Hill

them between his big paws, he could stop them from leaving him alone in the compound. It didn't work, however, because each time he did it, Ace and John spent less time with him. He soon stopped.

They had now been at Leith Hill for about three months. Christian was getting bigger, and the compound was starting to lose its attraction for him. He was getting bored again, and Ace and John worried about how much longer he could stay in the compound.

On 12th August, 1970, Christian celebrated his first birthday there and Unity made him a meat birthday cake. Before he ate it, they all made a wish that Christian would soon be in Kenya.

CHAPTER 8
WAITING

To get through the long wait that lay ahead of them, Ace and John decided to start preparations for Christian's eleven-hour flight to Kenya. For a start, Christian would have to travel in a special box. They would have to put him into the box at Leith Hill and then drive him to the airport in it. He would be inside it for at least fifteen hours. When Bill was trying to arrange everything with the airline on the telephone, the person he was talking to said: 'Flying a lion from England to Africa? You must be joking! Lions *come* from Africa!'

Ace and John phoned several zoos for advice. What was the safest way for their lion to travel such a long distance? They received a lot of different advice. Many people who were used to moving animals around the world weren't very interested in the animals' comfort. In the end, Ace and John decided to order a box that Christian could sit up in and turn around in. When the box arrived, they put it in Christian's compound so he could get used to it. He got into it for a few minutes every day.

The airline told them the price for flying Christian to Kenya depended on his weight, so they had to weigh him. It wasn't easy. They borrowed a weighing machine from the man at the meat market – who was finding his customers from Leith Hill even more of a mystery now! Christian weighed 80 kilos.

Ace and John had always wanted to see Christian's parents, so one day they went to the zoo where the two lions lived. Butch, Christian's father, and Mary, his mother, were the most beautiful lions they had ever seen. They thought that Christian looked very like his handsome father. But although the lions looked healthy, the place where they were kept was awful. Their cage was very small and all the lions could do was walk up and down on the cold stone floor, never stopping. Ace and John compared Christian's future to the life of his parents and felt very sorry for Butch and Mary.

Ace and John also tried to find Christian's sisters. Somebody thought they had been sold to a circus but nobody really knew. In those days it wasn't easy to find a lion's family. Now, in order to help protect animals, zoos keep more careful records. Ace and John had mixed feelings about zoos. They knew that zoos did important scientific studies to help protect animals in danger. But they also felt that the animals in them weren't usually happy. They often lived in small cages with cold stone floors, when what they needed was space and light and warmth.

Ace and John talked to Bill and Virginia a lot during those weeks of waiting. They learned that making the film *Born Free* had completely changed Bill and Virginia's lives. It had made them realise the value of wildlife. It had made them understand how important it was to take action to protect wild animals, before it was too late. Ace and John's relationship with Christian was having a similar effect on them too. They were beginning to learn how people have damaged the natural world and how competition for land, food and water has chased animals away from their homes. Ace and John knew that if they wanted things to change, they would need to do something about it.

After waiting so long at Leith Hill, Christian got too big for his travel box, so they had to order a new, bigger one. More weeks passed and then, just when they thought nothing was ever going to happen, a message arrived from George Adamson. He had found a place for Christian. Christian would leave England in a few days – his new life in Africa was about to begin.

CHAPTER 9
CHRISTIAN GOES HOME

The big day had finally arrived. At 3.30 pm on 22nd August, 1970, Christian was led into his travel box. This time, it wasn't just for a few minutes, but for at least fifteen hours. Ace and John gave him some meat which contained sleeping pills. Then they put the box in the van that would take him to Heathrow Airport. Unity came to Leith Hill to say goodbye to him.

Bill and Virginia travelled to the airport in their car, with Ace, John and Christian following them in the van. At the airport, the van drove straight to the plane and parked beside it. The pills seemed to be working: Christian was very relaxed in his box. At 5.30 pm, the box was lifted into the plane. It was a terrible moment. It was possible that Christian could die on the long journey, and Ace and John knew that they might never see him alive again.

The plane took off at 7 pm with Ace, John, Bill and the film team on it. Christian was in the luggage area. When the plane stopped in Paris, Ace and John were allowed to visit him. They found him sleepy and calm. Everything was fine so far, but the longest part of the journey was still ahead of them.

The plane landed in Nairobi, Kenya at 7 am. Ace and John waited nervously for Christian's box to be taken out of the plane. He had survived. At last he was able to leave his box and he greeted them with affection. His sleeping pills had lost their effect now – he wasn't calm any more, but nervous and exhausted. Still, at least he was in Kenya. After all the delays and problems, he had escaped life in a zoo. He was safely home in Africa.

George Adamson was at Nairobi Airport to meet them. He was very short with grey hair and a little beard. His eyes were very blue and he seemed to examine Ace and John carefully. Later, George said that while he had great confidence in working with Christian, he was very unsure about Christian's owners at first! He admitted feeling doubtful about them when he saw their long hair and strange, colourful clothes. It was only when he got to know Ace and John better that he changed his mind. He saw that there was a lot of deep affection and trust between them and Christian. He knew it would be very hard for them to leave Christian. Ace and John understood that there were many dangers in the wild, and that their lion would have to face these dangers alone.

Christian at the airport

Christian had to stay in a special compound at the airport for two days, until he felt fit enough to travel again. The area they were going to was called Kora. It was 450 kilometres north-east of Nairobi. It was a very dry area, a long way from anywhere. Few Africans lived there and the area was full of dangerous tsetse flies*. The Kenyan government had offered it to George because nobody else wanted it. They said the film company could use this unattractive piece of land for £750 a year.

* Tsetse flies feed on the blood of humans and animals. They carry dangerous illnesses.

Bill and George decided to break the journey into two parts. It would give the people at the camp more time to prepare for their arrival. It would also be easier for Christian – he would get less tired on shorter trips.

Bill, George, Ace and John left Nairobi early in several Land-Rovers*. Christian travelled with George. Christian was uncomfortable and walked up and down the seats. The group stopped often so that Ace and John could talk to Christian and give him water. George warned them that if they took Christian out of the vehicle, he might run away and never come back. Ace and John felt very proud when they called Christian back, and he jumped into the vehicle again immediately.

As the day went on, it got hotter and drier and the countryside became emptier and emptier. After driving about three hundred kilometres, they arrived at the camp where they would spend the next two nights. A small compound had been built for Christian. Ace and John led him into it and put their two beds in there too. He immediately climbed onto one of the beds and fell asleep. That was how he spent his first night in the wild!

Over dinner, George told Ace and John about the other lions he was going to return to the wild with Christian. One was Katania, a four-month-old lioness someone had found and given him. The other was Boy, a seven-year-old lion who had led an extraordinary life. He and his sister, Girl, had been found as cubs by an army officer. They lived their first year with the army. When the officer went back to the UK, he gave Boy and Girl to Joy and George Adamson. The cubs were used in the film *Born Free*. Then they were returned to the wild. Three years later, Joy found Boy again. He was very thin and he had a lot of

* Land-Rovers can travel across rough ground.

injuries. Joy and George looked after him. Now he was well again and George was going to return him to the wild with Christian. At the moment, the lions were at Joy Adamson's house in another part of Kenya. George was going to collect Boy from there soon.

The next morning Christian had his first walk in Africa. The countryside was empty. There were no trees, only thorn bushes. Christian walked quietly, stopping from time to time to take a thorn out of his paw. He seemed to know how to do that instinctively. Ace and John felt sure that he would soon get used to living in his natural environment.

Late in the afternoon, a gombi* came towards the camp. When Christian saw it, he immediately began to hunt it. George was worried. The young lion had no experience with such large animals and he could easily get hurt. George jumped into his Land-Rover and drove between Christian and the gombi. The gombi ran off and Ace and John caught Christian to put him in the Land-Rover. For the second time in his life he looked angrily at them and showed them his teeth. Ace and John let him go immediately.

George told them that Christian's instinctive following of the gombi was a good thing. He explained to Ace and John how Christian had cleverly hidden in a good position behind the bushes. The wind was coming towards him so the gombi could not smell him. 'Christian will be fine in the wild,' he said.

They set off the next day to cover the remaining 150 kilometres to Kora. The road was rough and they had to drive very slowly. As they got nearer, the countryside became greener. They began to see trees and bushes and

* A gombi is a large African cow.

animals. Africa began to come alive. They passed a village where people were wearing colourful African clothes and jewellery.

They arrived at the camp late in the afternoon. It was beautiful. The tents were under trees beside the Tana River and Christian's compound was near them. George left to collect the other lions from his home and was away for several days. While they waited for him to return, Ace and John had a wonderful relaxing time. In the mornings, before it got too hot, they went for walks with Christian. Later they went swimming in the river, although sometimes there were crocodiles there. Christian just sat under a tree and watched.

Ace, John and Christian at the Tana River

Christian seemed happy and free. He continued to be very gentle. He still liked to jump into Ace and John's arms to greet them. He nearly knocked them over, now that he was so large! Soon, the other lions would arrive. Ace and John hoped they would make Christian's life in the wild even more complete.

CHAPTER 10
KAMPI YA SIMBA –
'THE CAMP OF THE LIONS'

While George was away, Terence, his brother, was building a new camp a bit further away from the river's edge. This was where George and his lions would move. George thought it was safer for the lions to live away from the river, away from hunters and crocodiles. The new camp was called Kampi ya Simba – 'the camp of the lions'. It would be built around a hill of large rocks, called Kora Rock. From this hill the lions would be able to get a good view over the countryside.

When George arrived with Boy and Katania, he went straight to the new camp. The two lions needed to rest after their long journey. Two days later, Christian was taken to the new camp to meet them.

George had explained that the lions would need time to get to know each other. It could take weeks or even months. Christian had spent a lot of time with humans. George had to be sure that he could establish a relationship with other lions. If he couldn't, he wouldn't be able to live in the wild.

Two compounds had been built side by side at the new camp, with a fence between them. Ace and John led Christian into one of the compounds. They saw Katania and Boy in the other one. Katania was a cute little lioness cub. Boy was a huge male. He stared at Christian. Christian looked away, confused and afraid. He hid behind Ace and John, pressing against their legs. Suddenly Boy ran towards Christian. Luckily the fence was between them. Christian was really frightened. Boy

Katania (left) and Boy

walked away. He seemed pleased that Christian was frightened.

George had warned Ace and John that there could be problems between Boy and Christian. They were both male, and Boy was a lot older than Christian. It was natural for the older lion to be the 'boss', and Boy would want Christian to be frightened of him and show him respect. As for Christian, he had just discovered that he was not the only lion in the world. It was bad luck that the first other lion he met was at least twice his size.

Boy ran at Christian several more times that day. Christian sat on Ace and John or else hid behind their legs, pretending to be asleep. Ace and John were worried that Christian wasn't showing any interest in the other lions, but George was pleased. He said that both Boy and Christian were behaving just as he had expected.

The next day, Katania came up to the fence. She was

obviously interested in Christian. Christian was definitely interested in her too but he was too nervous to move closer.

The following morning George made a hole in the fence between the two compounds. Katania was the only lion who could get through it, so she could be with either Boy or Christian. If Katania became friends with Christian, it might help Boy and Christian's relationship too.

Ace and John took Christian for a walk that afternoon. He seemed pleased to be away from Boy and Katania. The countryside around the camp was grey and brown. Except for a few small thorn bushes and large rocks, it was dry and empty. It wouldn't be an easy area for the lions to live in. In a strange way, Christian had come to another 'World's End'.

The next day Christian met Katania. George led Boy out of his compound and Ace and John took Christian inside it. Christian went up to Katania confidently and touched heads with her gently. He licked and smelled her again and again. Boy watched jealously from outside as they played together.

When Boy was led into Christian's empty compound, Katania ran through the hole in the fence to him. Boy could smell that she had been near Christian and he showed his teeth angrily. But another important step had been taken.

That night, George thought it would be a good idea if Boy moved into the compound with Ace and John. He wanted Boy to spend some time with them before meeting Christian, so Christian was moved to another compound. Ace and John were very nervous. They didn't know what Boy might do. He was also much bigger and older than Christian and he had had a lot of injuries. He

Boy runs towards the fence.

was dangerous. But when Boy decided he wanted to sleep in their tent, Ace and John were too scared to argue with him!

The following day George decided that it was time for Boy and Christian to meet outside the compound. This was the moment they had all been scared of. They knew that if there was a fight between Boy and Christian, Christian could be badly injured or even killed.

Ace and John led Christian up to Kora Rock while George led Boy and Katania up from a different direction. Boy and Katania lay down about fifteen metres from Christian. Christian stared at them. He instinctively knew that, as he was not the 'boss', he should not make the first move. Everybody watched and waited. Twenty minutes went by.

Finally Katania went over to Christian and they touched heads. Immediately, Boy jumped up and ran towards Christian, with a loud roar. It was a very frightening moment. Christian lay on his back with his paws in the air. It was the right thing to do. He was showing Boy that he accepted him as boss. Boy lay down again a few metres away. But about ten minutes later Katania went up to Christian again and the same thing happened. Boy ran towards Christian again. This time, when Boy walked away, Christian looked very unhappy. He had a few cuts and he was walking with some difficulty.

George said afterwards that Christian had shown a lot of courage. He hadn't run away from Boy, but stayed to face him. It was a very good sign. There would be more tests like this if Christian wanted Boy to accept him.

It was an important moment for their relationship. Over the next few days, Christian followed Boy around and stayed as close to him as he could. If he got too close, Boy chased him away, but Boy was less violent than before. Christian copied all Boy's movements. He sat down when Boy sat down, and lay down in the same way. He still played with Katania sometimes but it was Boy who he really wanted to be with. When the three lions were together, Boy and Katania were always close but Christian was always a few metres away. He was not yet part of the family.

Ace and John were getting to know the other lions better. Soon Boy began to greet them in the same way that he greeted George – by touching his head against theirs. All three lions often spent the night in the tent with Ace and John. Katania bit their toes or stole their bed covers. Christian hid under the bed. Boy roared like thunder.

Filming continued. Christian was very easy to film. Ace and John put him where he needed to be and he stayed there. Boy was very difficult. He only did what *he* wanted to do and sometimes it took hours to get him in the right

Christian preferred to jump across the river rather than swim.

place. Ace and John thought Boy was a very handsome lion but they didn't much like his personality. When they described Boy as a 'wonderful' lion it was mainly because they were very glad that he hadn't eaten them!

Christian had now been in Africa for several weeks and was growing into a very beautiful animal. He had always been healthy, but one day he suddenly became ill. George took his temperature. He said Christian had tick fever*. Luckily, he was able to give Christian some medicine. George told Ace and John that he thought Elsa, the lioness who appeared in the book and film *Born Free*, had died

* Tick fever is an illness carried by small insects called 'ticks'. It can be very serious.

from tick fever. If the medicine had existed then, he might have been able to save her.

Now that Christian had been introduced to Boy, the film-making team decided to return to England to work on the film. George suggested that Ace and John should also leave Kora for a while. He said Christian needed to get used to life without them. So Ace and John decided to visit other parts of Kenya and Tanzania, before returning to Kampi ya Simba to say a last goodbye to Christian.

CHAPTER 11
TIME TO SAY GOODBYE

Ace and John were away from Kora for two weeks. They visited the Maasai Mara in Kenya, and the Serengeti, Lake Manyara and the Ngorongoro Crater in Tanzania. They saw lots of wild animals and birds. They also saw people like the Maasai who continued to live as they had lived for centuries, even though competition for their land was increasing. It was in the Maasai Mara that they saw their first lions in the wild. Ace and John were worried that these lions didn't seem very wild. They didn't seem to mind the Land-Rovers driving around them with tourists hanging out of their windows taking photographs.

Finally, they returned to Kampi ya Simba. They arrived late at night and were looking forward to seeing Christian.

John, Ace and Christian at Kora

But to their disappointment, he was missing. It was the first time he hadn't come back with Boy and Katania. George was worried, too. Within a few minutes, however, Christian came running into the camp. He jumped on Ace and John – he was so excited to see them. George thought that Christian must have known instinctively that Ace and John were back. Some people believe that lions can 'feel' things that other animals, including humans, don't know about.

Christian looked very well and George's relationship with him was obviously growing. George told them that one night he had made the mistake of making Christian a drink from dried milk powder. Christian had always loved this drink when he lived in London. Now, every night, he followed George around the camp. He knocked his head against George's legs until George gave him his bedtime drink of dried milk.

It was disappointing to learn that Boy had still not totally accepted Christian. Sometimes Christian seemed very unhappy about it. He and Katania were now quite friendly and George thought that perhaps Boy was jealous.

George told Ace and John about something that had happened while they were away. He was following the lions one morning when they saw a rhino. Boy and Katania moved well away from it, but Christian began to follow it, getting closer and closer. Suddenly, the rhino turned and ran towards him. Christian jumped into the air and over a bush, then he ran as fast as he could. George laughed but he said he hoped Christian had learned his lesson.

Boy had spent several nights away from the camp. He was beginning to look for an area to establish his home in the wild. On several nights they heard a wild lion roaring. Boy very cleverly chose the opposite direction to search for a place to live. It was impossible for one lion to establish a home, so George was planning to bring two other lionesses to help him. The lionesses, called Monalisa and Juma, were about Christian's age. Some African farmers wanted to kill them for attacking their animals, but George had offered to take the lionesses to Kampi ya Simba.

Ace and John loved talking to George. He told them about his life in India, where he was born in 1906, when his father was in the British army. After an English education, he had come to Kenya to work for the Department of Wildlife. He had been back to England only once since he'd left school, so he was interested to hear how London had changed. George also talked of

George Adamson with Ace, John and Christian

his love for wildlife. He had begun to realise a long time ago that many animals were in danger and he wanted to protect them. He loved lions most of all. They were proud animals who were able to give a great amount of love and trust. He believed that it was possible to communicate with them in a very special way that is not possible with other animals.

George felt that Boy would soon accept Christian, and with Katania, Monalisa and Juma, they would make a family. George was sure that they would all be returned to the wild soon. Ace and John were really happy. They could never have imagined or dreamed of a better result. After a journey of thousands of kilometres, Christian was where he belonged. But at the same time, they couldn't imagine life without him. Would they ever see him again?

CHAPTER 12
LETTERS FROM AFRICA

Several months after Ace and John had left Kora and returned to London, in January, 1971, they received a letter from George. The letter contained some very bad news.

```
12 January, 1971
Kampi ya Simba, Kenya

One evening last month, the lions went off
for several days, as they often do. This
time, however, Christian came back alone.
I thought Katania must be with Boy, but
the next morning Boy came back alone too.
Christian seemed to be as worried about her
as I was. After several days' searching,
I found paw prints belonging to all three
lions by the side of the river. On the
other side of the river I found only Boy's
prints. I think that Katania followed Boy
into the river but the water was moving too
fast for her. Lions are very good swimmers,
but Katania was still very small and light.
The water must have carried her down the
river. Poor little Katania was probably
eaten by a crocodile. It's very sad, and I
think Boy and Christian miss her very much.
```

But the letter went on to give some happier news as well.

```
You'll be pleased to hear that Boy and
Christian are now good friends and Boy
often greets Christian first these days!
```

And Christian has begun to roar! Boy and
Christian have met two wild lionesses.
One day when Boy and Christian returned
to camp, they weren't at all hungry. This
probably means that the lionesses had
killed an animal and they had all eaten
well. It's a good sign for the future of
this lion family.

Christian at Kora

George finished his letter by talking about Juma and
Monalisa, the two other lionesses he had agreed to rescue.
He said that he hoped to collect them soon. They were
fourteen months old – old enough to have experience of
hunting with their mother. He thought they would be a
great help.

Bill Travers flew out to Kenya soon after, and he also wrote to Ace and John on his return to the UK.

Let me tell you first of all that Christian is alive and well. He hasn't had a day's sickness since his tick fever. He's much heavier than he was. He is as tall as Boy. Christian is still very affectionate, and touches his head against George's whenever they see each other. Christian's coat is thinner and smoother, better suited to the hot weather. He looks wonderful. I think he will be the biggest lion in Africa.

Boy and Christian are the best of friends, and now, Juma and Monalisa have arrived. They are just the right age for Christian – only a few months younger than him. Their mother taught them to hunt, and Christian is going to learn a lot from them.

I am sure that you must think about Christian every single day. Let me tell you the last memory I took with me as I drove away from George's camp.

I looked in my mirror and saw the three friends. They were standing happily outside the gate, watching my Land-Rover drive away to the big city. I saw Christian press his head against George and then walk over to greet Boy and perhaps play some lion game.

I felt strangely happy. If people like you and George didn't exist, Christian would have had a very different life.

All the best,
Yours,
Bill

CHAPTER 13
REUNION

George now had four lions: Christian, Boy and the two lionesses, Monalisa and Juma. Surprisingly, after all the difficulties they had had at the beginning, Christian and Boy became the best of friends. They liked to spend all their time together, especially after the death of Katania. In the book about his life that he wrote in 1985, George Adamson described those days in Kora with Boy and Christian as some of the most enjoyable in his life. But everything was about to change.

The wild lions in Kora didn't like having four new lions in *their* area. Boy was the only adult lion and the head of the family. The wild lions attacked him often. One day he returned to camp with deep cuts on his back. George took him into the compound to look at his injuries. The wild lions waited outside. When they couldn't get Boy, they attacked and killed Monalisa.

Boy seemed to be in a lot of pain and he often went off on his own. George was worried about him. He was also worried about Juma and Christian, who had become good friends. They needed Boy to protect them and he wasn't there. But soon George was given two eighteen-month-old lionesses from a park in Nairobi. He called them Mona and Lisa in memory of Monalisa. He was also given a young male lion called Supercub. His lion family was growing at last.

Then something terrible happened. On 6th June, 1971, George heard Boy drinking water outside the compound. Then he heard cries coming from the same direction. He picked up his gun and ran out. He saw Boy holding

George's assistant, Stanley, in his mouth. George shouted and Boy dropped Stanley. George shot Boy dead and ran to help Stanley. But he was too late. Stanley was dead.

George couldn't believe that such a terrible thing had happened. He had warned Stanley not to go outside the compound, but on this occasion Stanley hadn't listened – and now he was dead. And one of George's favourite lions was dead too – a lion he had known ever since it had been a cub.

The 'accident' was reported in the international news. The local police and the Department of Wildlife came to ask questions. They said George was putting people's lives in danger. He was told he would have to close the camp. But there were many people in the Kenyan government who agreed with what George was doing. They also thought it was good for tourism in Kenya. In the end, Kampi ya Simba was allowed to continue.

Ace and John had been hoping to fly to Kenya to visit Christian and do more filming. After the awful news, they delayed their visit. Then, a few weeks later, they returned to Kora. It had been a year since they had seen Christian. They felt instinctively that he couldn't have forgotten them.

Ace described the reunion in a letter he wrote to his parents at the time.

Nairobi, 20 July, 1971

It was very hot and the lions were about a kilometre away from the camp. We had to wait several hours for it to be cooler. Finally, we walked in the direction of the lions, with the film team. We waited at the bottom of Kora Rock while George went up and called Christian. Soon after, Christian appeared at the top, about 75 metres away from us. He stared at us for a few seconds, and then slowly moved closer for a good look. He stared at us for ages. He looked wonderful, and up on the rocks, he didn't appear much bigger. We couldn't wait any longer and called him. He immediately started to run down towards us. He was HUGE! He jumped all over us, but he was very gentle. The three lionesses came up to us too, and Supercub, the little five-month-old male.

George says Christian is a really good-tempered lion – the best he's ever known. He's friendly to both humans and lions. He's healthy and beautiful and his front teeth are about 4 centimetres long! He's heavy, too. He was about eighty kilos a year ago ... now George thinks he's about twice that weight. Since Boy died, Christian's been the head of the family and he's very proud of himself. George is very pleased with his lions. He thinks they're a very close family and that they could begin to hunt quite soon. It's necessary if they're going to survive.

Ace and John stayed at the camp for a few days. They were woken every morning by Christian's roars. He was only two years old but his roars were deep and loud. They walked with the lions in the morning and went again to look for them in the afternoon. Now that Christian was the head of his family, they gave him more respect.

Reunion in Kenya, 1971

They did what *he* wanted to do. If he wanted to play, they played. If he wanted to show affection, they showed affection. If he wanted to be alone, they left him alone.

One day, Christian was leading them all on a walk when he suddenly ran off into the countryside with a big roar. He was chasing Mona and Lisa. They had been hiding, waiting to jump on Ace and John for fun. But it could have been very dangerous if Ace and John had shown fear or been knocked over. Christian was protecting them.

Kampi ya Simba was now much more established. George's brother, Terence, had built several little 'houses'. One of these was George's office, where he kept the radio telephone – his only connection with the outside world. This was where he also wrote, and there were books, letters, diaries and photographs. There was also a machine to provide electricity for the freezers which were full of meat for the lions.

It was wonderful for Ace and John to visit Kampi ya Simba but they only planned to stay a few days. They knew it was better for the lions not to be with humans too much. They had to learn not to trust humans or depend on them if they wanted to exist alone in the wild.

And yet, Christian had welcomed them in the most loving and affectionate way. It was a day that they would never forget. And they would have been surprised to know that almost forty years later, their experience would be shared by millions of people all over the world on *YouTube*.

Ace and John were sad to leave Christian, but he was obviously happy. When they left, their small plane circled the camp. Christian and the lions looked up from Kora Rock as Ace and John waved to George. They still had so many deep feelings for Christian. In this difficult and dangerous place, how long would he be able to survive?

CHAPTER 14
THE LAST GOODBYE

In January, 1972, two important letters arrived from Kampi ya Simba. The first was from George.

> I have been very lucky to find a young man to work with me at the camp. His name is Tony Fitzjohn. He's twenty-seven. He has done a lot of different jobs in his life and he seems to have lots of different skills. I think he's going to be a great help to me here.

Later, Tony himself wrote to Ace and John.

> I just wanted you to know how much I have grown to love Christian. I am amazed at how well he has learnt to survive in the wild and at the same time remain so affectionate.

In later letters from George, the news was not so good.

> Without Boy, Christian is finding it difficult to protect his family. A wild lion killed little Supercub. The lionesses, Juma, Mona and Lisa, have joined the wild lions, and Christian is all alone. He often has fights with the wild lions and comes back with injuries. The injuries are always on his front legs and shoulders, which tells me that he is fighting with great courage.

George and Tony thought Christian might never be able to establish a family in Kora. He seemed lonely and unhappy. And that made him dangerous. One day he jumped on George and knocked him over. He held George with his paws and took George's head in his mouth. Christian soon realised he had 'broken the rules' and he let go of George quickly. But one of his claws cut George's arm. Soon after that Christian knocked Tony down. He hit him with his paws and pulled him along by his head. Tony hit Christian hard on the nose. Luckily Christian let him go immediately so Tony was not badly hurt.

Ace and John were very upset when they heard these stories. Christian could easily have killed George or Tony. In August, 1972, they asked George if they could visit him and Christian, and meet Tony. George was very pleased

John (left) and Ace with Christian at Kora

but he warned them that they might not see Christian. To escape from the wild lions, he had had to go further up the Tana River and was often away for weeks.

When Ace and John arrived at the camp Christian was not there, but George said he had heard him not far away. He was with a wild lioness. Christian didn't appear until the third night. He didn't jump on Ace and John this time, but he greeted them with great affection.

Christian had become extremely big and strong. George thought he was possibly the largest lion in Kenya. He was only three years old and he probably weighed about two hundred and fifty kilograms. He would continue to grow and get heavier.

Ace wrote to his parents during their visit.

We see Christian every morning and evening for a walk and a chat. He is much calmer and more confident than last year. It's wonderful to be with him. He still likes to play games but he's huge. He still jumps on us but he does it extremely gently. He was taller than me and he licked my face. John nearly fell over when Christian tried to sit on his knees!

Ace and John got to know Tony during their visit. They had liked him immediately when he met them in Nairobi and they saw that Christian had accepted him completely. Tony didn't want Christian to be lonely and unhappy, so he was going to get a younger male lion from the park in Nairobi to keep him company. Tony was good at so many things. One of them was technology, and he was able to improve the camp's communications with the world.

Ace and John spent more time outside the camp on

this visit. Terence took them fishing and he showed them all the different plants in the countryside around the camp. Inside the camp they read George's reports to the Department of Tourism and Wildlife. These were a day-by-day record of the lions over several years. The reports said a lot about Christian and his return to the wild. In the past, George had been told that he wasn't 'scientific' enough. Scientific or not, George had probably discovered and written more about lion behaviour than anyone else in the world.

Ace and John went back to London. They stopped in Nairobi to show the film *The Lion at World's End* to people who knew George and who valued his work. Kampi ya Simba was expensive and the film helped to raise money. When they were back in London, Tony visited them and brought them news of Christian. He said that Christian and the wild lions had made peace. They weren't exactly friends, but they just roared to one another and left each other alone.

The bad news he brought was that some farmers had moved into the area. Christian had killed some of their animals, and Tony was sure that the farmers would try to kill Christian. There were also hunters in the area who killed animals for their skins and body parts. It was possible that things could get difficult for Christian.

In early 1973, George saw Christian in another area, on the other side of the Tana River. He was travelling north in the direction of the Meru National Park – a much more attractive area and a good place for hunting. It was safer from farmers and hunters too. That was George's last sighting of Christian.

Ace and John waited for news of him but none came. They liked to imagine that he established a large family and lived for another ten years. He had gone back to Africa, returned to the wild, and survived the most dangerous years. Together with George and Tony, they had done all they could for him. Christian had become a big, strong, healthy lion and his return to the wild was a complete success.

Christian at Kora

EPILOGUE

No one can be sure how long Christian survived in the wild. However, during his time at Kampi ya Simba, George had seen Christian with several wild lionesses, so he must have been the father of several cubs. Those cubs would one day have their own cubs. So Christian had a natural family. And then there was his second family, the family that George had put together: Boy, Katania, Juma, Monalisa, Supercub, Mona and Lisa. Juma and Lisa had cubs with wild lions and their cubs would have cubs too.

By the late 1970s, George knew there were enough lions in the area. He didn't want to add any new ones. If he did, there would not be enough animals for them to hunt. He spent his time working on the book about his life.

Kora became a National Park in October 1973. This meant George and his lions had government protection. George saw Kora as the special place of the 'cheerful, courageous young lion from London'. George continued to live at Kampi ya Simba until 1989. One day one of his guests was attacked on the road by hunters. The hunters shot George when he ran out to help.

George added a great amount to the world's knowledge about lions. He also made a big difference to wildlife protection in general and made people think about it in new ways. Since Christian's time, the number of lions in Africa has gone down by two-thirds. In 1988, the George Adamson Wildlife Preservation Trust (GAWPT) was established to fight to protect animals and Tony Fitzjohn became its first director.

John belongs to GAWPT and gives talks about their work around the world. In addition, he writes about travel and wildlife for newspapers and magazines. In 2008, he

produced a film called *Mkomazi: The Return of the Rhino.*
It was about moving four black rhinos from South Africa
to Tanzania. He and Ace have also been working with
GAWPT on a plan to rebuild the Kora National Park. After
George's murder, nobody took much interest in the Park
and it wasn't looked after.

Ace returned to Australia and began working with
Australian Aboriginal* art. This was a natural step for him
to take. Ace and John had bought lots of wooden bowls,
paintings and jewellery when they were in Africa and
they began to collect it. When Ace got home he wanted to
know more about the first people who lived in Australia,
and explore their art.

The *YouTube* video in 2007 made Ace and John
remember and relive their time with Christian almost
forty years earlier. They looked at all the old photographs
and films, reread all their letters, and fell in love with
Christian all over again. They still can't believe they had
actually returned a lion to Africa. It was an amazing thing
to do.

Ace and John are proud to have known George. They
saw at first hand the extraordinary deep understanding
and communication he had with lions.

Forty years later, George Adamson's work is still
continuing, even if he is not here to see it himself.
The story of a lion called Christian reminds us of the
relationship between all living things. It reminds us how
urgent it is to do something to protect wildlife before it is
too late. If everyone came together and took action with
the same courage that Christian showed us, imagine how
much we could achieve … .

* Aborigines are the native people of Australia.

CHRISTIAN AND THE

In 1971 the story of Christian the lion was well known. Ace and John's book, *A Lion Called Christian*, was very popular and the film, *The Lion at World's End*, was shown on TV around the world. But after a few years, the story was forgotten. Things would have stayed that way if it wasn't for the video-sharing website, YouTube.

'A CRY FOR AFRICA' ★★★★★

In 2006, a Californian student called Lisa Williams posted the clip of Christian's first reunion with his owners, Ace and John, on YouTube. She had seen the film about Christian and she wanted other people to see the clip. 'I couldn't believe it wasn't already on the Internet,' she said. Suddenly, Christian became an international phenomenon, as millions of people watched the clip and sent it to their friends.

Now there are lots of different versions of the clip, many with music and subtitles. They have been watched by over 60 million people.

Ace and John, now in their sixties, are amazed by the huge amount of interest in the video clip. They hope it will help to protect species in danger.

'We see it as our gift to the world,' they said. 'It's a cry for Africa from Christian, from almost forty years ago. It's a wonderful way for people to remember him.'

You Tube™ PHENOMENON

You Tube™ – WEBSITE OR PHENOMENON?

YouTube started in February, 2005. It was the idea of three men in California who wanted a website where people could post, view and share video clips. It first became really popular with a joke rap clip called 'Lazy Sunday' from a US TV programme, *Saturday Night Live*.

Several film and TV companies have attacked YouTube for breaking copyright law. As a result, YouTube has taken many steps to protect copyright. They have to keep clips to a maximum length of ten minutes.

YouTube is free, but it costs around one million dollars a month to run. It survives with money from business people and adverts.

Do you watch video clips on YouTube? What kind of clips are most popular with you and your friends?

OTHER You Tube™ STORIES

SUSAN BOYLE ★★★★★

Susan Boyle was a middle-aged woman who became famous overnight when she sang on the British TV show *Britain's Got Talent* in April, 2009. Susan lived a very quiet life in a small village in Scotland, and she looked very ordinary. People were amazed at the difference between her appearance and her beautiful singing voice.

Within ten days, YouTube and other Internet sites had had 100 million hits for Susan Boyle from all over the world. This was an Internet record.

What do these words mean? You can use a dictionary.
advance   clip   copyright   phenomenon   hit

77

ANIMALS IN

In 1969, Ace and John walked into a department store and bought a lion cub. In those days, it wasn't unusual to buy a wild animal. They could have bought a baby elephant or even a baby crocodile!

Laws were passed to stop people from buying and selling wild animals, but there are still thousands of animals in captivity in the world – in circuses, zoos and safari parks. What is life like for them there? Is it better than life in the wild?

A performing bear, India, 2003

CIRCUSES

A circus in Monte Carlo, 2003

Wild animals are used in circus acts all around the world. The Great British Circus, the biggest circus in the UK, still uses wild animals, including elephants and lions in its shows. There has been a lot of opposition to these shows. However, circus director, Martin Lacey, says that all their animals live in excellent conditions and are relaxed and happy. 'The Great British Circus welcomes the opportunity to show how these animals are really kept. People can see and judge for themselves,' he says.

See all sides of the story at:
www.captiveanimals.org
www.greatbritishcircus.co.uk
www.zsl.org

CAPTIVITY

SAFARI PARKS

Woburn Safari Park, UK, 2008

Safari parks have existed for many years in Africa as a way for visitors to see animals in the wild. In safari parks, animals and people have changed places: the animals walk around freely, while the visitors stay in their cars and watch the animals from there.

The first safari park outside Africa was Longleat Safari Park in England, which opened in 1966.

> **How important do you think freedom is for animals? Or is 'freedom' a very human idea?**

ZOOS

Zoos have existed for over 3,000 years. In the past, the animals were kept in small cages with cold, stone floors. These days, living conditions for zoo animals have improved greatly: they are given good food, and often live longer than animals in the wild.

Lions at London Zoo, 2009

Scientists are able to study them and help animals in the wild, and some breeding programmes in zoos actually help to save endangered species.

On the other hand, not all species are suited to life in a zoo. Lions and other big cats, for example, can't walk around freely or hunt as they would in the wild, and they can become stressed and unhappy. Unfortunately, these are the animals that people want to see the most.

> **What do these words mean? You can use a dictionary.**
>
> captivity elephant bear
> conditions breeding
> species stressed

ANIMALS IN DANGER

One in every five species of mammals in the world are in danger of becoming extinct. The animal trade is big business. It is worth between six to ten billion dollars every year. Animals are killed for their skins, which are used in clothing and furniture, their bones and horns, which are used in Asian medicines, and their meat. The land that many animals live on is also being used more and more for building or farming.

Do you know of any other animals in danger? Why are they dying or being killed? What can be done to help these animals survive? What can you do?

GORILLAS are in danger because the forests where they live in central Africa are being destroyed by farmers and tree companies. Gorillas are also hunted for their meat. A few gorillas, especially babies, are caught alive and sold as pets. The laws to protect gorillas have had little effect, but now 'gorilla viewing' has become a big tourist attraction. This could provide local people with a new way of earning money.

Find out more at:
www.bornfree.co.uk
www.georgeadamson.org
www.wildlifenow.org
www.savetherhino.com

BLACK RHINOS are almost extinct. When Ace and John visited Tanzania in 1970, there were over 7,000 black rhinos in the country. Today there are less than 100. Rhinos are killed for their horns, which can sell for thousands of pounds. The horn is used for special knives and also in traditional Chinese medicine. It is against the law to buy and sell rhino horn, but hunting still goes on.

SNOW LEOPARDS used to be killed for their skin but recently, increasing numbers are being killed for their bones, which are used in traditional Chinese medicine. Snow leopards are often killed by farmers because the leopards kill their farm animals for food.

TIBETAN ANTELOPES are small antelopes that live in the high mountains of Tibet and China. Fifty years ago, there were one million of them. Now there are fewer than 75,000 and their numbers are becoming smaller every year. Farmers are moving into their area and taking their land to mine for gold. Antelopes are also killed for their soft – and expensive – wool.

What do these words mean? You can use a dictionary.
mammal species extinct trade traditional horns

SWINGING

The late '60s and early '70s were a time of great cultural change in Britain and America. There were big changes in music, fashion and young people's lifestyles. London was right at the centre of these new trends and quickly became known as 'Swinging London'.

FASHION

London was the heart of fashion. Top designers opened shops on Carnaby Street and the King's Road in Chelsea, and these areas became famous. This was the time of bell-bottomed trousers, platform shoes and the Mary Quant* mini-skirt.

Two women outside a boutique on the King's Road in Chelsea, London, 1969.

After England won the football World Cup in 1966, the British flag, the 'Union Jack', became fashionable. People wore Union Jack coats, dresses, skirts and even underwear!

'Granny Takes a Trip' was a boutique on the King's Road (1966 – mid-1970s). It has been called the 'first psychedelic boutique in London'.

What do these words mean?
You can use a dictionary.

boutique   psychedelic   demonstration
feminist   protest

* Mary Quant was a famous fashion designer in the 1960s and '70s.

LONDON!

MUSIC

After the success of The Beatles and The Rolling Stones in the late '60s, Jimi Hendrix became the face of the '70s.

1970: Rock star Hendrix dies after party

Rock star Jimi Hendrix has died after a party in London. A number of sleeping pills were found at his house.

Hendrix, 27, was born in the USA, but became famous in Britain with his band The Jimi Hendrix Experience.

WOMEN'S RIGHTS

Life was very different for women before the 1970s. It wasn't until 1971, for example, that Swiss women even got the right to vote! Women wanted to be equal with men in every area of their lives. Feminist books and magazines appeared for the first time.

In 1970, feminists protested against the 'Miss World' beauty competition, held in London. They said that the competition showed women as attractive objects only.

WAR AND PEACE

In the early '70s, the peace movement of the '60s grew stronger and there were a lot of demonstrations, especially against the unpopular war in Vietnam*. John Lennon's song 'Imagine' expressed the mood that many people felt at the time.

What is similar about the '70s and the time we are living in now? What are the differences?

* The Vietnam war (1959 – 1975) was a war between North and South Vietnam. Many US soldiers were sent to fight with South Vietnam.

PROLOGUE & CHAPTERS 1-4

Before you read

You can use your dictionary for these questions.

1 Match the words with the definitions.

cub   damage   greet   hug   reunion   roar

a) a young lion or other wild animal

b) the sound a lion makes

c) a meeting with someone again after a long time

d) say hello or welcome someone in a friendly way

e) put your arms around someone

f) harm or break something

2 Are these sentences true or false? Correct the false ones.

a) Cats, dogs and lions all have **paws**.

b) Horses and lions have sharp **claws**.

c) The **basement** is at the top of a building.

d) **Pumas** belong to the 'big' cat family, like lions.

e) A **circus** is a place where you go to see motor racing.

3 Complete the sentences with these words.

affection   cage   lick   lion   respect

a) You ... the stamp in order to make it stay on an envelope.

b) Many zoo animals are kept in a small ... .

c) Some people think children have less ... for older people these days than in the past.

d) The little girl showed her ... for her baby sister by giving her a ... on her cheek.

e) The ... is called the king of all wild animals.

After you read

4 Answer the questions.

a) Why are these months or years important to the story? What happened then?

May, 1969   August, 1969   December, 1969   1971   2007

b) What were some of the problems Ace and John needed to face? How did they face them?

c) What was Christian's daily routine once he got used to his new home?

d) What was Christian's personality like? What adjectives are used to describe him? What things did / didn't he like to do?

e) What was Christian's relationship like with …
   the cleaner?   customers in the shop?   children?   Unity?
   Ace and John?

f) What were some of the things Christian did 'professionally' outside his home?

5 What do you think?
   a) Do you think Ace and John were right to buy Christian? Why / why not?
   b) Which parts of the letter (on page 27) do you think were right? Which were wrong?

6 Writing
   Ace often writes letters to his parents in Australia.
   Write his letter to them the day after Christian arrived at their flat.
   Describe what happened yesterday (and last night) when they brought Christian home.

CHAPTERS 5-9

Before you read

7 Complete the sentences with these words.
   **caravan   compounds   crocodile   instinct   slow-motion
   tent   thorn**
   a) You sleep inside a … when you go camping.
   b) A … is a small mobile house that can be pulled behind a horse or vehicle.

c) I got a sharp … in my finger when I picked some flowers.

d) It's a lion's … to follow a wild animal and kill it to eat.

e) The zoo consisted of several large … where the animals were kept safely, away from humans.

f) In order to see clearly who the winner of the race was, the cameras played the film back in … .

g) A … is a big animal with sharp teeth, that lives near the water and is highly dangerous.

8 Guess the answers. Then read and check.

a) What kind of problems will Christian (and his owners) have as he gets bigger in London?

b) Will it be easy to organise his return to the wild in Africa? What difficulties could there be?

After you read

9 Number these sentences in the correct order.

a) Ace and John watched Bill's film about three lions who had been returned to the wild.

b) Bill introduced Ace and John to the director of *Born Free*, James Hill.

c) Bill contacted George Adamson in Kenya to tell him about Christian.

d) Bill suggested making a film about Christian to pay for his return to the wild in Kenya.

e) Ace and John met the actors, Bill Travers and Virginia McKenna, in April, 1970.

f) Bill and Ace were all invited to dinner at Bill and Virginia's house in the country.

g) The film would be called *The Lion at World's End*.

h) Ace and John introduced Bill and Virginia to Christian and told them their worries about his future.

10 Only one of these sentences is true. Which one? Correct the false sentences.

   a) Christian had to wait several months to go to Africa because the flights were fully booked.

   b) There were no problems during the first two days filming of *The Lion at World's End* in London.

   c) Life was much easier for Christian when he moved to Bill and Virginia's house in the country.

   d) Ace and John got lots of helpful advice about safe ways for animals to travel long distances.

   e) The journey to their final destination, Kora, was a fifteen-hour flight, followed by a two-hour drive.

   f) Kora was a lovely area with a lot of people, 45 kilometres south-west of Nairobi.

11 What do you think?

Ace and John spent a lot of time and money organising Christian's return to Africa. Do you think it was worth it? What would you have done with a lion cub who turned into a huge lion?

12 Writing

Imagine you are George Adamson.

Today you met Christian with Ace and John at Nairobi Airport. Write a short letter to a friend. Describe what happened and how you felt about both the lion and the two men.

CHAPTERS 10-14 & EPILOGUE

Before you read

13 Circle the word that is different from the others. Why is it different?

   a) rhino   puma   lion   crocodile   thorn

   b) fence   roar   cub   claw   paw

14 Guess the answers. Then read and check.
  a) What difficulties will Christian face as he prepares to return to the wild?
  b) Will he find it easy to make friends with other lions?

After you read

15 Fill in the missing steps in their relationship.
When Christian first met Boy in August 1970, Boy ran towards him and Christian was really frightened.
By January 1971, Boy and Christian were good friends.
What happened in between?

16 Answer the questions.
  a) George Adamson successfully returned many lions to the wild. What happened to the ones in this story? What happened to ... Boy? Katania? Juma? Monalisa? Mona? Lisa? Supercub?
  b) What do you learn about George Adamson from this last part of the book? What were some of his lasting achievements?
  c) Who was Tony Fitzjohn? In what ways did he help George?
  d) Ace and John visited Kora three times, in 1970, 1971 and 1972. How were their visits different each time?

17 What do you think?
George last saw Christian in early 1973, travelling north towards Meru National Park – a safe and attractive area. What do you think happened to him after that?

18 Writing
If Christian had been able to write a diary, what would the entries be for ...
... the day he first met Boy and Katania at the Kampi ya Simba?
... the day of his YouTube reunion with Ace and John in 1971?